DOG TRAINING
WITH
MR PERKS

Mr Perks would like to thank the Editor of *The Shooting Gazette* for giving him his first big break

DOG TRAINING
WITH
MR PERKS

BRYN PARRY

SWAN·HILL
PRESS

This book is dedicated to Emma
with thanks for everything.
I am also grateful to Mango, Pickle and Toffee
for all their help and technical advice.

First published in the UK in 2006
by Swan Hill Press, an imprint of Quiller Publishing Ltd

British Library Cataloguing-in-Publication Data
A catalogue record for this book
is available from the British Library

ISBN 1 904057 93 4
  978 1 904057 93 2

Printed in China

Swan Hill Press
An imprint of Quiller Publishing Ltd
Wykey House, Wykey, Shrewsbury, SY4 1JA
Tel: 01939 261616 Fax: 01939 261606
E-mail: info@quillerbooks.com
Website: www.countrybooksdirect.com

CONTENTS

Introduction   7

Chapter 1   History of the Dog   8
Chapter 2   Choosing the Ideal Dog   24
Chapter 3   Welcoming the New Puppy   40
Chapter 4   Basic Training   56
Chapter 5   Advanced Training   68
Chapter 6   Field Trials   94
Chapter 7   Diet and Grooming   100

INTRODUCTION

Iam extremely grateful to Mr Perks and of course, the lovely Mrs Perks, for this book. Mr Perks is well known in the Gun Dog world and for years his regular page in *The Shooting Gazette* has been essential reading for anyone interested in dog training.

Mr Perks should be considered to be the leading authority in the subject and probably would be if only his dogs would do what he told them. Undaunted by constant set-backs, the extraordinarily patient Mr Perks continues to issue training commands, sure in the certain knowledge that his students will one day achieve canine perfection.

It has been a privilege to work with Mr Perks and a joy to see his techniques at first hand. His maxim of 'it's all very well in practice but will it work in theory?' is so apt and should be an inspiration to all us aspiring trainers.

I should at this stage acknowledge the hard work, devotion and loyalty shown by Mr Perks' canine students… but I won't.

Bryn Parry

HISTORY OF THE DOG

THE MODERN DOG IS RELATED TO THE WOLF

DOGS BECAME DOMESTICATED THOUSANDS OF YEARS AGO . . .

. . . WHEN THEY BECAME MAN'S HUNTING PARTNERS

THE ANCIENT EGYPTIANS WORSHIPPED A DOG GOD . . .

THE GREEKS DEPICTED THEM AS MESSENGERS OF THE GODS

IN TIBET, MASTIFFS WERE TRAINED AS TEMPLE GUARDS

THE ROMANS USED WAR DOGS

DURING THE TANG DYNASTY, EMPEROR MING MARRIED A PEKINESE

BONAPARTE FORBID ANYONE NAMING THEIR DOG NAPOLEON

Dogs have tended our flocks . . .

GUARDED OUR HOMES . . .

Acted as guide dogs . . .

HELPED TO SAVE OUR LIVES . . .

Been used to seek out drugs

AND SERVED GALLANTLY IN OUR ARMED FORCES

CHOOSING THE IDEAL DOG

A GOOD HIP AND EYE SCORE IS IMPORTANT

LABRADOR PUPPIES
READY NOW
EXCELLENT PEDIGREE
KC Reg
Sire FTC   Dam's father FTC
SPECIAL OFFER

INSIST ON SEEING THE PUPPY'S MOTHER

SOME BREEDS TO CONSIDER . . .

SPRINGER SPANIEL

COCKER SPANIEL

GOLDEN RETRIEVER

LABRADOR RETRIEVER

IRISH SETTER

FLAT-COATED RETRIEVER

GERMAN WIRE-HAIRED POINTER

ITALIAN SPINONE

English Pointer

IRISH WATER SPANIEL

Curly-Coated Retriever

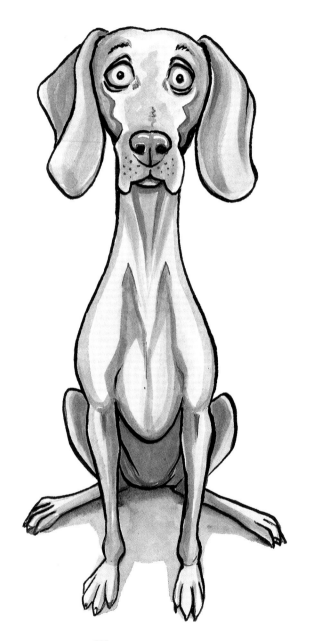

WEIMERANER

WELCOMING
THE
NEW PUPPY

A HOT WATER BOTTLE CAN COMFORT A NEW PUPPY

A PUPPY WILL GIVE YOU LOVE . . .

. . . AND THE OCCASIONAL MESS

PUPPIES NEED A ROUTINE

A RADIO CAN PROVIDE COMPANY

A healthy puppy looks forward to meals

PUT DOWN PLENTY OF NEWSPAPER

MR PERKS
DUNTRAININ
BONETON
DOGSHIRE
SP12K9

YOUNG PUPPIES ARE NATURALLY CURIOUS

PROVIDE TOYS TO PREVENT BOREDOM

THE PUPPY'S NAILS SHOULD BE TRIMMED

PUPPIES LOVE BALL GAMES

First impressions are important

INTRODUCTION TO OTHER PUPPIES HELPS DEVELOP SOCIAL SKILLS

YOUNG PUPPIES HAVE A STRONG URGE TO CHEW

BASIC TRAINING

TRAINING THE WORKING DOG

FIRST, ENSURE YOU HAVE THE DOG'S UNDIVIDED ATTENTION

ALL TRAINING SESSIONS SHOULD HAVE CLEAR GOALS

THE DOG MUST RESPOND TO HIS MASTER'S VOICE

THE PUPPY WILL LEARN TO SIT TO THE UPTURNED HAND

THE DESIRE TO FOLLOW THE TRAINER IS VERY STRONG AND MUST BE RESISTED

THE DOG WILL SOON LEARN TO RECOGNISE BASIC HAND SIGNALS

THE PUPPY WILL LEARN TO RESPOND TO THE STOP WHISTLE - EVEN WHEN EYE CONTACT IS BROKEN

'HI LOST'

THE DOG WILL SOON BECOME FAMILIAR WITH THE MASTER'S COMMANDS

NO DOG SHOULD BE INTRODUCED TO THE FIELD UNTIL IT HAS BECOME ABSOLUTELY RELIABLE AT HEEL

A break can be beneficial

ADVANCED TRAINING

THE DOG CAN BE TESTED FOR GUN SHYNESS BY A SUDDEN CLAP OF THE HANDS

THE PUPPY WILL LEARN TO ENJOY HIS LESSONS WITH THE DUMMY

THE DOG MUST LEARN TO TURN TO THE WHISTLE

THE DOG MUST LEARN TO DROP TO SHOT

THE DOG MUST LEARN TO WORK UNDER COVER

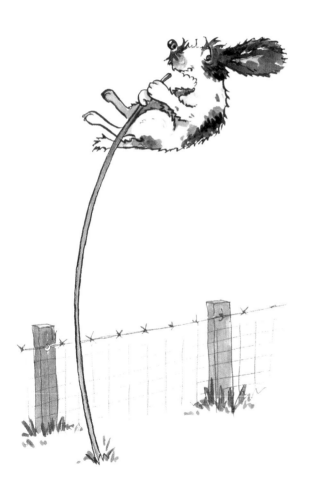

THE DOG SHOULD JUMP WITH CONFIDENCE

REMEMBER, WIND CAN AFFECT THE DOG'S PERFORMANCE

OBEDIENCE PROBLEMS CAN BE SOLVED BY A JERK ON THE LEAD

THE DOG MUST SIT STILL ON THE PEG

FUR SHOULD BE IGNORED

GOOD HANDS ARE VITAL

THE DOG WILL SOON BE ABLE TO MARK A BIRD

SHOT GAME IS FOOD AND MUST BE TREATED AS SUCH

ABSOLUTE SILENCE IS THE RULE . . .

ELECTRIC COLLARS ARE DISCOURAGED

THE WHISTLE IS THE BEST FORM OF COMMUNICATION IN THE FIELD

WHEN TAKING GAME FROM A DOG NEVER LIFT THE HEAD

EVERY EFFORT SHOULD BE MADE TO PICK UP ALL THE BIRDS

SOME BREEDS HAVE A STRONG INSTINCT TO HUNT

THE DOG MUST BE PROPERLY PREPARED BEFORE BEING INTRODUCED TO WATER . . .

89

THE DOG WILL SOON BECOME CONFIDENT AT WATER RETRIEVES

TRAIN THE DOG TO JUMP STREAMS

THE DOG MUST LEARN TO ENDURE THE COLD AND WET

ENSURE THAT THE DOG'S BEDDING IS WARM AND DRAUGHT FREE

FIELD TRIALS

FIELD TRIALS CAN BE AN ORDEAL

GAME MUST BE PROPERLY PRESENTED

A GOOD DELIVERY MUST BE REWARDED

A STARTING PISTOL CAN BE USED FOR TRAINING

Reward success

DIET AND GROOMING

A GOOD DIET IS ESSENTIAL FOR AN ENERGETIC PERFORMANCE

The menu reads:

MENU

Noisettes of Prime Beef Nestling on a Bed of Pork Chops with a Drizzle of Gourmet Gravy

Dogs need a varied . . .

. . . AND WELL BALANCED DIET

EXCESS WEIGHT IS UNHEALTHY

EXERCISE THE DOG DAILY

ENSURE THE DOG HAS ACCESS TO DRINK

CLEANLINESS IS NEXT TO GODLINESS

THE DOG MUST BE KEPT WELL GROOMED

BRUSH YOUR DOG'S TEETH DAILY

REGULAR TRIPS TO THE VET ARE IMPORTANT

PILLS CAN BE HIDDEN IN FOOD

REGULAR FLEA TREATMENTS ARE VITAL

A WELL TRAINED DOG IS A HAPPY DOG